MAKING BABIES

First published in the United States of America
in 1974 by the Walker Publishing Company, Inc.

Published simultaneously in Canada by Fitzhenry &
Whiteside, Limited, Toronto.

ISBN: 0-8027-6171-2

Library of Congress Catalog Card Number: 73-15267

Printed in the United States of America.

"In this edition the color plates are reproduced in black
and white in order to avoid a price increase."

Photo Credits:
p. 19—Dr. Landrum B. Shettles
pp. 21, 23—Lennart Nilsson, TIME/LIFE Picture Agency
p. 35—Walter Chandoha

MAKING BABIES

An Open Family Book For Parents And Children Together

by Sara Bonnett Stein

in cooperation with
Gilbert W. Kliman, M.D.
Director

Doris Ronald
Educational Director,
The Cornerstone Nursery-Kindergarten

Ann S. Kliman
Director,
Situational Crisis Service

Phyllis Schwartz
Community Coordinator

The Center for Preventive
Psychiatry
White Plains, New York

photography by Doris Pinney
graphic design, Michel Goldberg

Walker and Company
New York, New York
Created by Media Projects Incorporated

A Note About This Book

When your child was a baby, you took him to the doctor to have him immunized for childhood illnesses. The injections hurt a little, but you knew they would prepare his body to cope with far more serious threats in the future. Yet there are other threats as painful and destructive to a child's growth as physical illness: Separation from his parents, a death in the family, a new baby, fears and fantasies of his own imagining that hurt as much as pain itself. These Open Family Books are to help adults prepare children for common hurts of childhood.

Caring adults try to protect their child from difficult events. But still that child has ears that overhear, eyes that read the faces of adults around him. If people are sad, he knows it. If people are worried, he knows it. If people are angry, he knows that too.

What he doesn't know—if no one tells him—is the whole story. In his attempts to make sense of what is going on around him, he fills in the fragments he has noticed with fantasied explanations of his own which, because he is a child, are often more frightening than the truth.

We protect children because we know them to be different, more easily damaged than ourselves. But the difference we sense is not widely understood. Children are more easily damaged because they cannot make distinctions yet between what is real and what is unreal, what is magic and what is logic. The tiger under a child's bed at night is as real to him as the tiger in the zoo. When he wishes a bad thing, he believes his wish can make the bad thing happen. His fearful imagining about what is going on grips him because he has no way to test the truth of it.

It is the job of parents to support and explain reality, to guide a child toward the truth even if it is painful. The dose may be small, just as a dose of vaccine is adjusted to the smallness of a baby; but even if it is a little at a time, it is only straightforwardness that gives children the internal strength to deal with things not as they imagine them to be, but as they are.

To do that, parents need to understand what sorts of fears, fantasies, misunderstandings are common to early childhood—what they might expect at three years old, or at five, or seven. They need simpler ways to explain the way complicated things are. The adult text of each of these books, in the left hand column, explains extraordinary ways that ordinary children between three and eight years old attempt to make sense of difficult events in their lives. It puts in words uncomplicated ways to say things. It is probably best to read the adult text several times before you read the book to your child, so you will get a comfortable feel for the ideas and so you won't be distracted as you talk together. If your child can read, he may one day be curious to read the adult text. That's all right. What's written there is the same as what you are talking about together. The pictures and the words in large print are to start the talking between you and your child. The stories are intense enough to arouse curiosity and feeling. But they are reasonable, forthright and gentle, so a child can deal with the material at whatever level he is ready for.

The themes in these Open Family Books are common to children's play. That is no accident. Play, joyous but also serious, is the way a child enacts himself a little bit at a time, to get used to events, thoughts and feelings he is confused about. Helping a child keep clear on the difference between what is real and what is fantasy will not restrict a child's creativity in play. It will let him use fantasy more freely because it is less frightening.

In some ways, these books won't work. No matter how a parent explains things, a child will misunderstand some part of the explanation, sometimes right away, sometimes in retrospect, weeks or even months later. Parents really can't help this fact of psychological life. Nothing in human growing works all at once, completely or forever. But parents can keep the channels of communication open so that gradually their growing child can bring his version of the way things are closer to the reality. Each time you read an Open Family Book and talk about it together, your child will take in what at that moment is most useful to him. Another day, another month, years later, other aspects of the book will be useful to him in quite different ways. The book will not have changed; what he needs, what he notices, how he uses it will change.

But that is what these books are for: To open between adult and child the potential for growth that exists in human beings of all ages.

A child can seem not to notice the things he notices most of all—the things that confuse him, that make him worried or very curious, that are not explained to him because people don't talk about them much. People don't talk much about sex. Maybe when they were children they were confused, worried, curious too. Maybe not much was explained to them. Still, not seeming to notice, a child forms ideas about what he sees and hears. He explains to himself, if no one else does, how come a girl has no penis, what dogs are doing when they "play," why a lady's belly has grown so large. His own explanations are sometimes scary. And they are usually wrong.

The pictures in this book are here to be noticed, talked about, explained. They are, simply, to make a distinction between what are the fantasies and what are the facts of life.

Children think about a lot of things. About how seeds grow. About how a baby grows.

They notice things that make them curious. Why is that cat's belly getting so fat?

What could it be that makes the cat's tummy look big? The cat is pregnant, but your child may think she only ate a lot.

When a child hears us talking about a baby growing inside us, he remembers something he has been told—that if he eats a lot, he will grow. We say "fat" about both pregnancy and obesity. We talk about big tummies whether it is a baby or a dinner inside. It is no wonder so many children think a baby is made by eating food. It is hard to clear up this misunderstanding with really young children, three or even four years old. But as you look together at this picture you can lay the groundwork by pointing to where in your own body a baby grows, and how different that is from your stomach, which is up under your ribs.

It is because the cat has baby kittens growing inside her.

If you have ever doubted that children, even toddlers, notice pregnancy, take a look from the child's eye level. It would be hard not to notice that belly. That's why, even if no questions are asked, it's best to remark—"It looks as though so and so is going to have a baby." If you are not open with your child about what he might already suspect, it is as though you were keeping something from him on purpose. Could it be bad? he wonders. Maybe you both know someone who is pregnant. This is a good time to talk about it.

A mother can get a fat belly too. There is a baby growing inside her. It is called being pregnant.

Children sometimes think being pregnant is being sick. They hear women talking about morning sickness; they listen to complaints of backache and heartburn. And more often than you would think, a child overhears people talking about birth in scary ways—difficult labor, pain, emergency. Since children have experience of going to the doctor when something's wrong, it is easy for them to put two and two together: Pregnancy is "something wrong." As you talk about this picture, help your child recall his own check-ups—how the doctor and you are both interested to see how he is growing, how strong and well he is.

It is okay for your child to know that pregnancy can be uncomfortable, but it is important that he feel it is good, natural, and not dangerous.

The mother goes to the doctor, but she is not sick. "The baby is growing nicely," the doctor says.

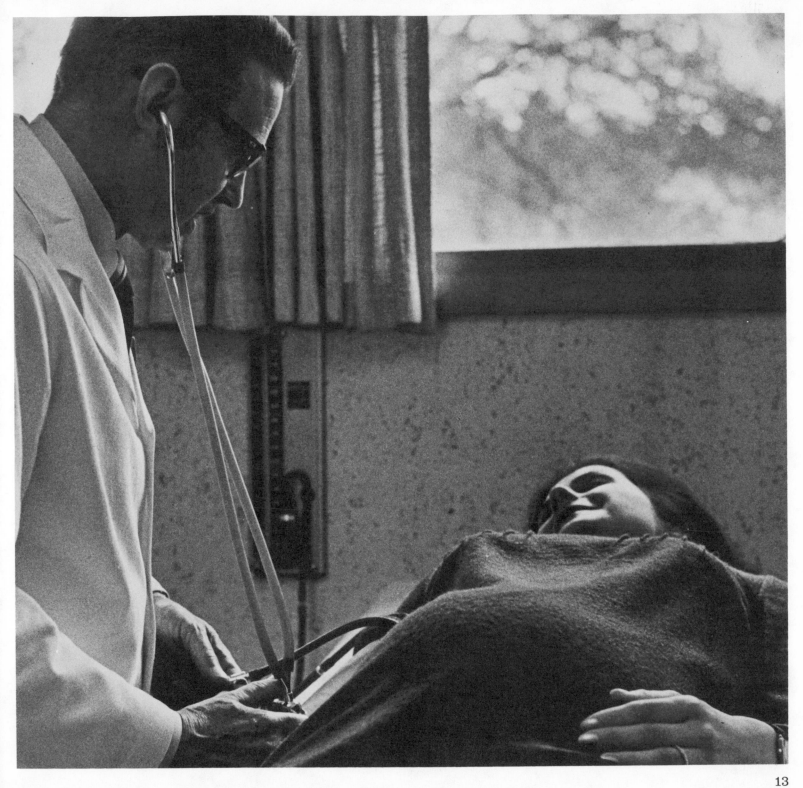

A little child's thinking is still so literal, so confined to what he has actually experienced, that the problem of how a baby gets out of his mother's uterus is very difficult. Some children think babies are born through the anus (rectum) —the only place from which they, after all, have ever pushed anything solid out of their bodies. One child thought the doctor cuts mommies open to get babies out. It is unwise to disagree entirely— this child had seen the incision from a caesarean on a mother dog. Your child may freely tell you his ideas. If he does, don't tell him he is wrong; just tell him how you think it happens. Your child may not tell you his ideas—perhaps he already suspects they are kind of funny. Tell him what you think anyway.

The boy feels the baby kicking inside his mother. But he is not sure how the baby will get out.

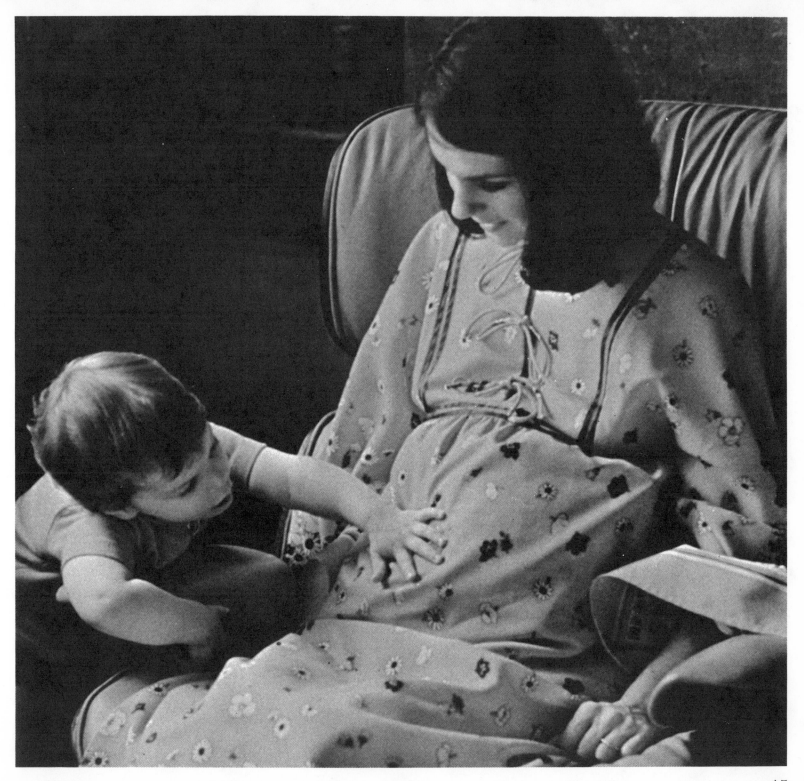

This is how the kittens are born. And how a baby is born too.

Birth is something children rarely get to see; and because it is often "a secret," they are both curious and worried. This picture shows kittens, still wet, just being born.

If your child has a lot of questions, here are some answers: The kittens were in a place inside the mother where babies grow. It is called a uterus. The kittens are wet because it was wet inside the uterus. It was warm and comfy, soft and spongy. The hole the kittens are coming out of is a special opening of the "tunnel" for babies —it is called a vagina. Getting born doesn't hurt the kittens. The cat is a little uncomfortable, but it is a good feeling to have babies and she wants to be a mother.

Talking about how spongy and comfortable the uterus is will help you to explain what often worries children—seeing menstrual blood. You can explain that your uterus gets ready for a baby to start by growing a spongy lining like pillows, with blood to make it soft. Then if no baby starts, the blood isn't needed and comes out through your vagina. The explanation will help your child understand that you are not bleeding from a cut— that it does not mean something awful has happened.

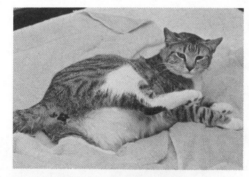

It is very difficult to explain sperm, ova and fertilization to a young child. It is too invisible; it is too mysterious. Even though it happens in us as adults, we cannot be said to experience fertilization. It is all right to tell your child about it, but he will probably not really understand until he is six or seven or even older. If he is perplexed, you can sympathize with him: "Doesn't it sound strange?" "I know it's hard to believe." "I've always had trouble understanding things I can't even see."

A baby starts
like this:
A sperm from
the daddy joins to
an egg inside
the mommy.
At first they are
almost too small
to see, but
they grow together
to be a baby.

It is also not easy for a child to accept that he was once so little, or so different. The pictures here and on the next page are to help your child with the idea that babies change and grow from the time they start until the time they are ready to be born.

Some children are very interested, some don't like the idea so much. If your child doesn't like it, agree that a person might feel that way about once looking so different. At this point, or anywhere else in this book that seems to make your child restless, squirming or distracted, be prepared to put Making Babies away until he wants to see it again.

This is how a baby looks when it is just starting inside its mommy. It is very, very little.

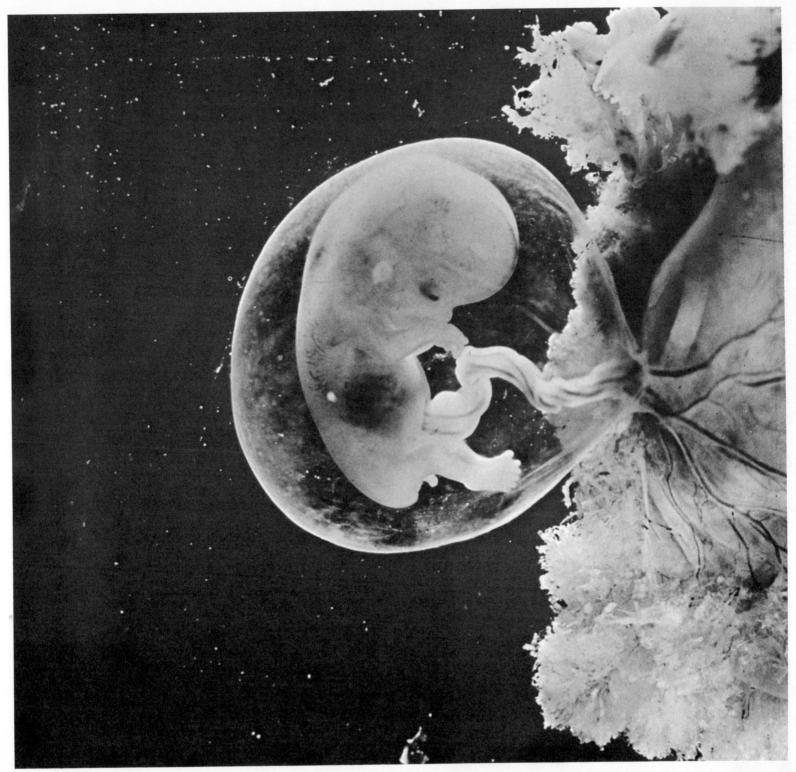

Your child will probably wonder about the umbilical cord. Explain that a baby is too young to know how to eat before he is born, so instead he gets what he needs through the umbilical cord. "See? Here is your belly button where you were once connected to your mommy."

The baby changes and grows.
Now it is almost ready to be born.

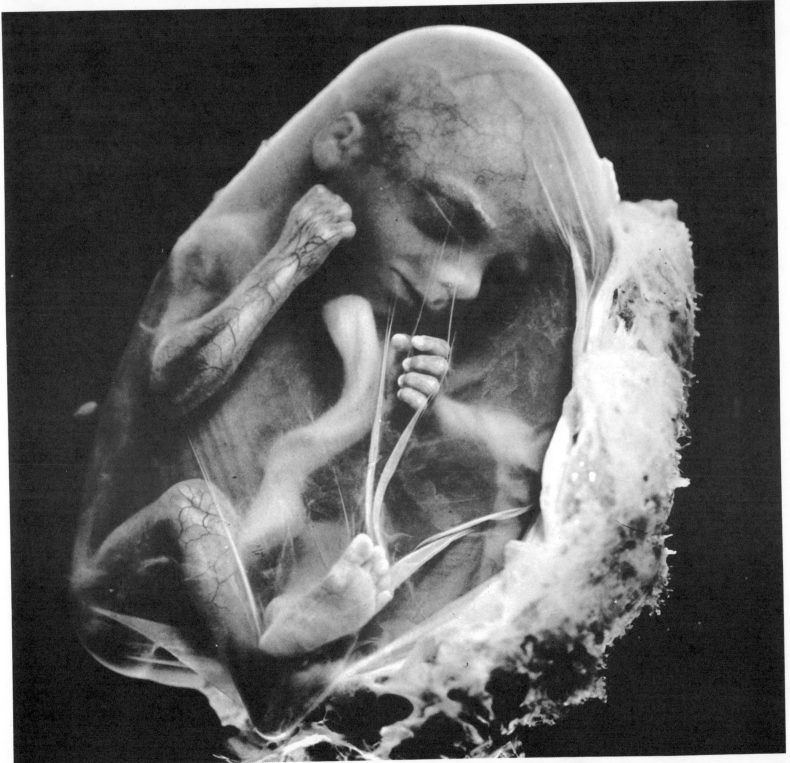

Your child can see that this new-born baby is a girl. And he can see that where the umbilical cord was is now her belly button.

A child needs to be sure that his body knows how to grow. His skin grows over a cut to heal it. A bone grows back together when it is broken. And even an unborn baby grows just the right way to become ready to be born.

As you look at the picture together, tell it as your child's own story—his history. He will want to hear about when he was in your uterus, and about his own birth. He would probably love to look through snapshots of himself and hear the story of how he grew.

And now
the baby is born!
All the time
she was inside
her mommy
she knew how
to grow to be
a baby girl.

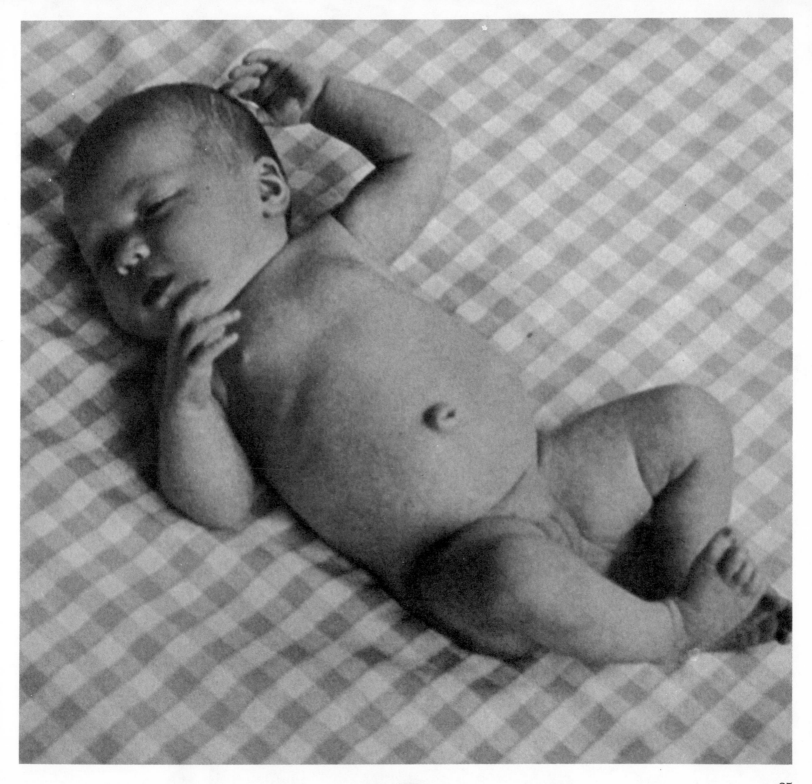

Children need to like the sex they are. But they get mixed up because they are not sure it is impossible to change. A boy likes his penis so very much that it is scary to see that girls don't have one. He hopes it is "very little"—hidden, but really there. And boys and girls both wonder: Do girls first have one and then lose it? Could they grow one some day? Could a boy lose his? Children don't usually tell people these fears and fantasies. Still, to be firm is to be reassuring: A boy is born a boy, and will grow to be a man. A girl is born a girl, and will grow to be a woman.

Some people are born girls, and some people are born boys.

Part of a child's liking the sex he is comes of his interest in his own body, in how it looks and what it can do. But he is curious too about other people's bodies. Perhaps he plays doctor so he can "examine" another child. Perhaps he likes to accompany other children to the bathroom to see what he can see. Sometimes these events, though they are common and natural, are embarrassing to adults. The pictures on this page and the next give a child a chance to look at other naked children at home, in privacy, for as long as he wants. It is a way of showing him it is all right to be curious and all right to ask about what he wants to know.

Children usually notice that males have a penis and testicles, but they may not notice that females have a clitoris and vagina. You may need to explain where they are, and that the vagina is a special inside place with an opening of its own. Let your child know her vagina and clitoris, or his penis and testicles, have good feelings in them.

Every girl has a vagina.

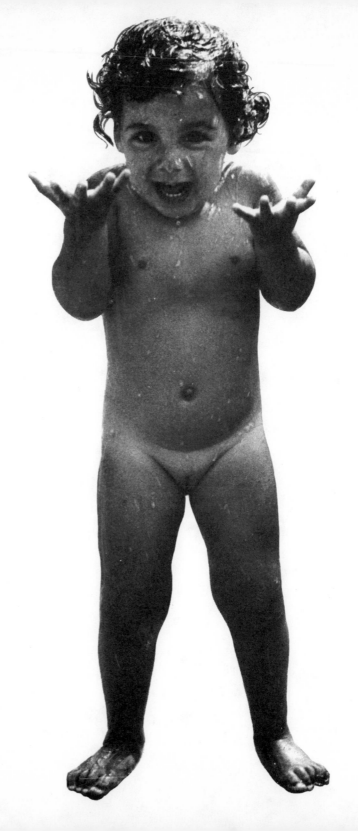

Every boy

has a penis.

Because there are limits to how much we can let a child investigate other humans, it may be helpful to let them observe animals. Dogs are a likely choice, not only because children have ample opportunity to notice their sexual differences, but because they often have ample opportunity to note their sexual behavior too.

It is the same with animals. Some dogs are girl dogs and have a vagina. When they grow up, they can be pregnant, and they can feed their babies milk through their nipples.

As girls become aware of sexual differences, they are sometimes sad that they have no penis—it looks like such a good, playful and powerful thing to have. It is important to tell your daughter that only girls have a vagina, only women can make milk for their babies and feed them through their nipples. It is hard for a little girl to wait so long to have breasts— reassure your daughter that like all growing, her breasts will grow when it is the right time.

Boys are sometimes sad they will not have breasts, because that seems decorative and important too. They may wish, and even play, that they are pregnant. It is all right to share regrets with both boys and girls—yes, it is too bad we don't have everything.

And some dogs are boy dogs and have a penis. When they grow up, they can help to start a baby dog.

It is easy to be shocked to really see a picture of dogs mating. But children have no particular reason to be shocked at mating unless adults act uncomfortable or evasive. Each of these pictures shows dogs enjoying each other's company in one way and another. Talk with your child about each one. If you get to one that bothers you, try not to slur over it. If more formal words like intercourse feel awkward, you can use "making love" to mean the same thing. Making babies is one way of loving.

These dogs are loving each other; they are starting puppies.

Some children think that dancing together, or kissing, or the magic words and special costumes of a wedding are how people start babies. It is nice that all these theories, however wrong, are on the right track: People being intimate together has lots to do with starting babies!

Unless your child has asked, you don't really have to go into the mechanics. Just read the text and gently turn the page. But if he is interested in the details, you can say, "The man puts his penis in the woman's vagina, so his sperm can go inside to join with her egg. And that's how people start babies." It is sensible and honest to add that, because it feels nice, people make love together even when they are not starting a baby.

This mommy and daddy are loving each other too. It feels warm and happy to them.

The wish to have a baby, the wish to be as intimate with another person as grownups can be together, is very strong in many children. It is hard to wait. Once in a while your child may act too grown up—stroking a breast, giving a sexy kind of kiss. Children do not do these things because they have "picked it up somewhere." They do it because they already feel some of the feelings we do. The feelings are natural; they are also confusing. Those ways of loving are for grownups, and it's best to say so.

A boy wishes
he could be a father.

Still, you can help your child to share his wishes—how he would like to have a wife, how she would like to have a husband of her own some day. You can talk about the time when your son or daughter will have babies, and how nice it will be to be a mother or a father, and how nice for you that you will be Grandma then, or Grandpa.

A girl wishes
she could be a mother.

43

Each of us in every generation has started from the same unseen beginning toward our birth; and through our growing, to our loving as man and woman, to start again another life's beginning. Those are the facts of life. If they are earthy as we tell them honestly, they are poetic as we share them openly, because it is these facts that tie us each to the other, and each to another generation. Your own child, little as he is, already holds the seed of the children he will have someday.

Once they were babies. Now they are children. And someday...

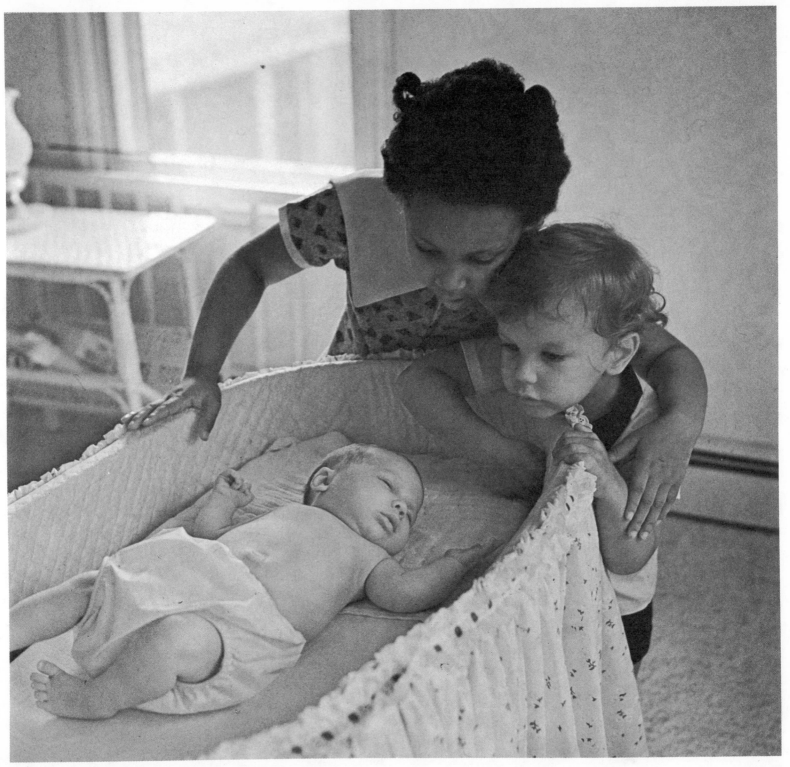

...they will all grow up.

DATE DUE